Who We

in Cnrist

The Two Kinds of Life

by

E. W. KENYON

SEATTLE WASHINGTON
KENYON'S GOSPEL PUBLISHING SOCIETY
1942

Hope. Inspiration. Trust.

WE'RE SOCIAL! FOLLOW US FOR NEW TITLES AND DEALS:
FACEBOOK.COM/CROSSREACHPUBLICATIONS
@CROSSREACHPUB

AVAILABLE IN PAPERBACK AND EBOOK EDITIONS
PLEASE GO ONLINE FOR MORE GREAT TITLES
AVAILABLE THROUGH CROSSREACH PUBLICATIONS.
AND IF YOU ENJOYED THIS BOOK PLEASE CONSIDER LEAVING A
REVIEW ON AMAZON. THAT HELPS US OUT A LOT. THANKS.

*From the book "The Two Kinds of Life",
originally titled "What We Are in Christ"*

Who We Are in Christ

I was surprised to find that the expressions "in Christ," "in whom," and "in Him" occur more than 130 times in the New Testament. This is the heart of the Revelation of Redemption given to Paul.

Here is the secret of faith—faith that conquers, faith that moves mountains. Here is the secret of the Spirit's guiding us into all reality. The heart craves intimacy with the Lord Jesus and with the Father. This craving can now be satisfied.

Ephesians 1:7: "In whom we have our redemption through his blood, the remission of our trespasses according to the riches of his grace."

It is not a beggarly Redemption, but a real liberty in Christ that we have now. It is a Redemption by the God Who could say, "Let there be lights in the firmament of heaven," and cause the whole starry heavens to leap into being in a single instant. It is Omnipotence beyond human reason. This is where philosophy has never left a footprint.

Our Redemption is a miracle of His grace. It is according to "the riches of his grace." It is a present-tense work wrought "through His blood." It is lavish. It is abundant. Our Redemption is a perfect thing. When you know it, enter into it, and your heart grows accustomed to it, there will be ability in your life that you have never known.

Colossians 1:13, 14: "Who delivered us out of the authority of darkness and translated us into the kingdom of the son of his love; in whom we have our redemption, the remission of our sins." You are delivered out of the authority of Satan. You are free. It is in Him that you have your Redemption. You have been delivered out of Satan's dominion. You have been "translated into the kingdom of the son of his love." You are free from the dominion of Satan.

The hour will come when you will awaken to the fact that he cannot put disease upon you, that he cannot give you pain and anguish in your body.

The hour will come when you will know that want and poverty are things of the past as far as you are concerned.

You will shout amid the turbulence and fear of other men "The Lord is my shepherd. I do not want. He makes me to lie down in plenty, in fullness. I am satisfied with Him."

This Redemption is real. Satan is defeated, disease is outlawed, and want is banished.

We are free. John 8:36: "If therefore the son shall make you free, you shall be free in reality." The word "indeed" really means "reality." John 10:10: "I came that they may have life, and may have it abundantly." What is Life? Life is the Nature of God. You may have the Father's Nature abundantly. You are "in Christ," in the Father's presence. You are in the very realm of life. This realm of Life has in it the Life that transcends reason. We have Eternal Life, God's very Substance. In John 14:6 Jesus said: "I am the way, the reality, and the life." He was unveiling His heart to us, showing what He can be to us in our daily life.

He can be all that His heart of love desires to be to those whom He has redeemed. He can be reality to us. How our hearts have craved this! He can fulfil every desire of our hearts. Galatians 5:1: "Stand fast therefore, and be not entangled again in a yoke of bondage." The gravest danger of the believer is the possibility of his lapsing back into bondage after he has been made free. He leaves the realm of the spirit and faith, and walks in the realm of the senses. As Sense Reason gains the supremacy he loses his joy in the Lord.

We are New Creations in Christ Jesus. We are just finding out what this can mean to us. II Corinthians 5:17: "Wherefore if any man is in Christ, he is a New Creation." This New Creation fact gives to you all that it means to Jesus and the Father whether you know it or not. Paul's revelation is filled with New Creation truth. It is God's dream for you to enjoy the fullness of this New Creation's privileges. "The old things are passed away." Those old things of bondage, fear, doubt, want, sickness, weakness, and failure are gone.

You say, "That is not possible." But it is. The New Creation is just like the Master. He is its head. He is the Vine, you are the branch. As He is, so are you. John 15:1-7: "I am the true vine, and my Father is the husbandman... I am the vine; ye are the branches."

As long as you deal in doubts and fears; as long as you sit in judgment on yourself, you will never arrive. You will never enjoy these things.

If; however, you will act on the Word—act on it as you would act on a letter from some friend, you will arrive.

When you read, "All things have become new," start thinking of yourself as living in this new realm.

You have been reconciled to God through Jesus Christ.

You have perfect fellowship with Him now.

Oh, the wealth that belongs to you in this new relationship! Dare to act your part.

Ephesians 2:10: "For we are his workmanship, created in Christ Jesus." If you are His workmanship, you are satisfactory to Him. He is pleased with you.

We have preached condemnation and sin so long that we do not know how to preach righteousness and to tell the people what they are in Christ.

When someone does tell them, they feel that it is false teaching. They feel that anything is false teaching that does not honor sin and lift it into the place of Christ.

You are God's new man. Ephesians 2:15 declares that He brought into being the new man: "Having abolished in his flesh the enmity, even the law of commandments contained in ordinances; that he might create in himself of the two one new man, so making peace." Ephesians 4:24: "And put on the new man, that after God hath been created in righteousness and holiness of truth."

The New Creation knows but one Lord. Jesus is the Lord of the New Creation.

Colossians 2.6,7 gives us a graphic statement of facts "As therefore ye received Christ Jesus the Lord, so walk in him, rooted and builded up in him, and established in your faith, even as ye were taught, abounding in thanksgiving."

What a glorious truth! No longer are you a weakling. His strength is your strength. We are so strong that we are to abound in thanksgiving. When we stop abounding in thanksgiving we deteriorate spiritually.

Psalm 27:1: "Jehovah is my light and my salvation; whom shall I fear? Jehovah is the strength of my life; of whom shall I be afraid?"

Psalm 23:1: "The Lord is my shepherd; I shall not want."

You swing free from the old prison house of bondage and fear and want, of hunger and cold. You are out in the freedom of God.

Hebrews 7:25 is Jesus' present attitude toward you: "Wherefore also he is able to save to the uttermost them that draw near unto God through him, seeing he ever liveth to make intercession for them." He ever lives to make intercession for you.

He is seated at the Father's right hand. Say it over, "He ever lives for me."

Just as the wife lives for the man whom she loves, so in a greater measure the Lord Jesus lives for you. He has only one business: that of living for you.

We are His Righteousness

Of all the wealth that is known to the human heart, there is nothing that equals this: that Jesus declares through the apostle Paul that we are His Righteousness.

I cannot grasp it. We are His Righteousness. How precious we must be to Him!

He once became our righteousness. He once declared us righteous by His resurrection from the dead. Now He goes beyond the declaration and makes that a reality. II Corinthians 5:21: "Him who knew no sin he made to be sin on our behalf; that we might become the righteousness of God in him." We have become the righteousness of God in Him. I Corinthians 1:30: "But of him are ye in Christ Jesus, who was made unto us wisdom from God, and righteousness and sanctification, and redemption."

Note these three blessed facts:

He becomes our righteousness. Romans 3:26.

He is made righteous for us. I Corinthians 1:30.

We have become the righteousness of God in Him. II Corinthians 5:21.

Galatians 2:20: "That life which I now live in the flesh I live in faith, the faith which is in the son of God, who loved me and gave himself up for me."

He loved me. He gave Himself up for me. What love is revealed here! He not only redeemed me and sanctified me, but now before heaven He says, "I am that man's Redemption. I am that man's sanctification."

Then I can hear His voice rise to notes of utter triumph when He shouts, "I am His Righteousness and His Wisdom."

This is all His work. It is not of man's works lest he should say, "I had a share in that." Your repenting, crying, and weeping had naught to do with your righteousness or your redemption. You stand complete in Him, in all the fulness of His great, matchless life.

Romans 8:33, 34 is the climax of the revelation of our Redemption: "Who shall lay anything to the charge of God's elect?" You are God's elect. Jesus and the Father have elected you and now He says, "Who shall lay anything to the charge of my own son or my daughter?" There is only one person of any standing before the Supreme Court who could lay anything to your charge. That is Jesus, and He will not do it.

"Who is he that condemneth? It is Christ that died, yea rather, that was raised from the dead, who is at the right hand of God, who also maketh intercession for us?" Can't you see the wealth of your position? Can't you see the riches of the glory of your inheritance in Christ? You are in Him. All that He planned in Jesus is a heart reality now.

There is no condemnation for you. There is no judgment for you. There is no fear of death for you. Why? Because death is simply swinging the portals open for you to march in triumph into the presence of your Father. I John 4:18 grips the heart: "There is no fear in love: but perfect love casteth out fear."

In Christ we have received Eternal Life, the Nature of our Father. That Nature is Love. That Love is perfect. Our human love is imperfect. His love is "agape," the love that makes life beautiful.

You may not perfectly understand or perfectly enter into it, but it is His perfect Love, and it is all yours now.

I Corinthians 12:12: "For as the body is one, and hath many members, and all the members of the body, being many, are one body; so also is Christ." We are so one with Him that we are called Christ. The Church is called the "Christ ones."

He is the Vine. You are the branch. John 15:1-8 (5th verse): "I am the vine, ye are the branches; he that abideth in me, and I in him, the same beareth much fruit." As the branch is to the vine, so are you to the heart of Jesus.

You are utterly one with Him. All this time you have been thinking about your sin, about your weakness, and your failings. Hear Him whisper to your heart now from Romans 8:1: "There is therefore now no condemnation to them that are in Christ Jesus."

If you are Born Again you are "in Christ." You are a conqueror. You are free from condemnation. You are the righteousness of God in Him. You are the fulness of God in Him. You are complete in Him. The wealth of His glory, the wealth of His riches, have never been sounded. You are righteous. There is no sin-consciousness for you. There is no inferiority complex for you. You are now in Christ, the very righteousness of God.

You can use the Name of Jesus without fear. You can do as Peter did in Acts 3:5, 6: "And he gave heed unto them, expecting to receive something from them. But Peter said, 'Silver and gold have I none, but what I have, that give I thee. In the name of Jesus Christ of Nazareth, walk.'" You can swing free. John 16:23, 24: "If ye shall ask anything of the Father, He will give it you in my name." John 15:7 is yours now: "If ye abide in me, and my words abide in you, ask whatsoever ye will, and it shall be done unto you."

You are in Him. He is in you. His Word abides in you. You are His Righteousness. You are His Life. You can do His works now. John 14:12, 13: "Greater things than these shall ye do, because I go unto the Father. And whatsoever ye shall ask in my name, that will I do, that the Father may be glorified in the son." You take your place. You use the Name to heal the sick. His death was not in vain. His suffering was not in vain. You stand complete in His completeness, filled with His fulness. You are filled with His holiness. His grace is yours.

Hebrews 4:14-16 can become a reality in you: "Having then a great high priest who hath passed through the heavens, Jesus the Son of God, let us hold fast our confession." The word here is not "profession" but "confession." Christianity is called "the great confession." Your confession is what you are in Christ. All that we have said to you is a reality. You hold fast to it.

The adversary will try to make you deny your confession. He will try to make you confess anything rather than this. He will try to make you confess weakness and failure and want.

But you hold fast to your confession: "My God does supply every need of mine." Philippians 4:19. You stand by that confession. Philippians 4:13: "I can do all things in him who strengtheneth me." You make the declaration that He is the strength of your life. Say it aloud to yourself until you get accustomed to hearing it.

I Peter 2:24: "Who his own self bare our sins in his body upon the tree that we, having died unto sins, might live unto righteousness; by whose stripes ye were healed." You died unto sins with Christ on that cross; you arose to walk in righteousness; and by His stripes you are healed. When Jesus arose from the dead, healing belonged to you.

Hold fast to your confession in the face of every assault of the enemy. You rebuke it in the Name of Jesus.

You walk in the Way of Righteousness, which means acting and living as though the Word was spoken to you by Jesus. That is the way of victory. That is the way where you cast out demons and disease in the Name of Jesus. Every disease that has afflicted a

Christian could have been healed if there had been anyone who had dared to walk in righteousness for that believer, who would have dared to walk in the fulness of his privileges in Christ. The devil could have been driven out and healing could have been his.

Hebrews 4:15,16: "For we have not a high priest that cannot be touched with the feeling of our infirmities; but one that hath been in all points tempted like as we are, yet without sin. Let us therefore draw near with boldness unto the throne of grace." You are invited to come now to the throne room and sit with the Master and with the Father.

You are to come boldly. Don't come creeping in. Don't come in confessing your sin, bewailing your weakness and failures. Put on the new garment. Dress fittingly to appear before the throne.

You are the sons and daughters of God Almighty without condemnation. You will find mercy and grace to help in time of need.

ABOUT CROSSREACH PUBLICATIONS

Thank you for choosing CrossReach Publications.

Hope. Inspiration. Trust.

CROSSREACH PUBLICATIONS These three words sum up the philosophy of why CrossReach Publications exist. To create inspiration for the present thus inspiring hope for the future, through trusted authors from previous generations.

We are *non-denominational* and *non-sectarian*. We appreciate and respect what every part of the body brings to the table and believe everyone has the right to study and come to their own conclusions. We aim to help facilitate that end.

We aspire to excellence. If we have not met your standards please contact us and let us know. We want you to feel satisfied with your product. Something for everyone. We publish quality books both in presentation and content from a wide variety of authors who span various doctrinal positions and traditions, on a wide variety of Christian topics that will teach, encourage, challenge, inspire and equip.

We're a family-based home-business. A husband and wife team raising 8 kids. If you have any questions or comments about our publications email us at:

CrossReach@outlook.com

Don't forget you can follow us on <u>Facebook</u> and <u>Twitter</u>, (links are on the copyright page above) to keep up to date on our newest titles and deals.

BESTSELLING TITLES FROM CROSSREACH[1]

A. W. TOZER

HOW TO BE

Filled

WITH

THE

Holy Spirit

CrossReach Publications

How to Be Filled with the Holy Spirit

A. W. Tozer

Before we deal with the question of how to be filled with the Holy Spirit, there are some matters which first have to be settled. As believers you have to get them out of the way, and right here is where the difficulty arises. I have been afraid that my listeners might have gotten the idea somewhere that I had a how-to-be-filled-with-the-Spirit-in-five-easy-lessons doctrine, which I could give you. If you can have any such vague ideas as that, I can only stand before you and say, "I am sorry"; because it isn't true; I can't give you such a course. There are some things, I say, that you have to get out of the way, settled.

GOD STILL SPEAKS

A. W. TOZER

God Still Speaks
A. W. Tozer

Tozer is as popular today as when he was living on the earth. He is respected right across the spectrum of Christianity, in circles that would disagree sharply with him doctrinally. Why is this? A. W. Tozer was a man who knew the voice of God. He shared this experience with every true child of God. With all those who are called by the grace of God to share in the mystical union that is possible with Him through His Son Jesus.

Tozer fought against much dryness and formality in his day. Considered a mighty man of God by most Evangelicals today, he was unconventional in his approach to spirituality and had no qualms about consulting everyone from Catholic Saints to German Protestant mystics for inspiration on how to experience God more fully.

Tozer, just like his Master, doesn't fit neatly into our theological boxes. He was a man after God's own heart and was willing to break the rules (man-made ones that is) to get there.

Here are two writings by Tozer that touch on the heart of this goal. Revelation is Not Enough and The Speaking Voice. A bonus chapter The Menace of the Religious Movie is included.

This is meat to sink your spiritual teeth into. Tozer's writings will show you the way to satisfy your spiritual hunger.

CLAIMING OUR RIGHTS

E. W. KENYON

Claiming Our Rights
E. W. Kenyon

There is no excuse for the spiritual weakness and poverty of the Family of God when the wealth of Grace and Love of our great Father with His power and wisdom are all at our disposal. We are not coming to the Father as a tramp coming to the door begging for food; we come as sons not only claiming our legal rights but claiming the natural rights of a child that is begotten in love. No one can hinder us or question our right of approach to our Father.

Satan has Legal Rights over the sinner that God cannot dispute or challenge. He can sell them as slaves; he owns them, body, soul and spirit. But the moment we are born again... receive Eternal Life, the nature of God,—his legal dominion ends.

Christ is the Legal Head of the New Creation, or Family of God, and all the Authority that was given Him, He has given us: (Matthew 28:18), "All authority in heaven," the seat of authority, and "on earth," the place of execution of authority. He is "head over all things," the highest authority in the Universe, for the benefit of the Church which is His body.

The Two Babylons
Alexander Hislop

Fully Illustrated High Res. Images. Complete and Unabridged. Expanded Seventh Edition. This is the first and only seventh edition available in a modern digital edition. Nothing is left out! New material not found in the first six editions!!! Available in eBook and paperback edition exclusively from CrossReach Publications.

"In his work on "The Two Babylons" Dr. Hislop has proven conclusively that all the idolatrous systems of the nations had their origin in what was founded by that mighty Rebel, the beginning of whose kingdom was Babel (Gen. 10:10)."—A. W. Pink, The Antichrist (1923)

There is this great difference between the works of men and the works of God, that the same minute and searching investigation, which displays the defects and imperfections of the one, brings out also the beauties of the other. If the most finely polished needle on which the art of man has been expended be subjected to a microscope, many inequalities, much roughness and clumsiness, will be seen. But if the microscope be brought to bear on the flowers of the field, no such result appears. Instead of their beauty diminishing, new beauties and still more delicate, that have escaped the naked eye, are forthwith discovered; beauties that make us appreciate, in a way which otherwise we could have had little conception of, the full force of the Lord's saying, "Consider the lilies of the field, how they grow; they toil not, neither do they spin: and yet I say unto you, That even Solomon, in all his glory, was not arrayed like one of these." The same law appears also in comparing the Word of God and the most finished productions of men. There are spots and blemishes in the most admired productions of human genius. But the more the Scriptures are searched, the more minutely they are studied, the more their perfection appears; new beauties are brought into light every day; and the discoveries of science, the researches of the learned, and the labours of infidels, all alike conspire to illustrate the wonderful harmony of all the parts, and the Divine beauty that clothes the whole. If this be the case with Scripture in general, it is especially the case with prophetic Scripture. As every spoke in the wheel of Providence revolves, the prophetic symbols start into still more bold and beautiful relief. This is very strikingly the case with the prophetic language that forms the groundwork and corner-stone of the present work. There never has been any difficulty in the mind of any enlightened Protestant in identifying the woman "sitting on seven mountains," and having on her forehead the name written, "Mystery, Babylon the Great," with the Roman apostacy.

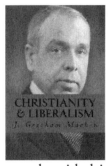

Christianity and Liberalism
J. Gresham Machen

The purpose of this book is not to decide the religious issue of the present day, but merely to present the issue as sharply and clearly as possible, in order that the reader may be aided in deciding it for himself. Presenting an issue sharply is indeed by no means a popular business at the present time; there are many who prefer to fight their intellectual battles in what Dr. Francis L. Patton has aptly called a "condition of low visibility." Clear-cut definition of terms in religious matters, bold facing of the logical implications of religious views, is by many persons regarded as an impious proceeding. May it not discourage contribution to mission boards? May it not hinder the progress of consolidation, and produce a poor showing in columns of Church statistics? But with such persons we cannot possibly bring ourselves to agree. Light may seem at times to be an impertinent intruder, but it is always beneficial in the end. The type of religion which rejoices in the pious sound of traditional phrases, regardless of their meanings, or shrinks from "controversial" matters, will never stand amid the shocks of life. In the sphere of religion, as in other spheres, the things about which men are agreed are apt to be the things that are least worth holding; the really important things are the things about which men will fight.

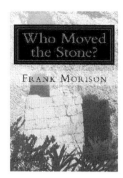

Who Moved the Stone?
Frank Morison

This study is in some ways so unusual and provocative that the writer thinks it desirable to state here very briefly how the book came to take its present form.

In one sense it could have taken no other, for it is essentially a confession, the inner story of a man who originally set out to write one kind of book and found himself compelled by the sheer force of circumstances to write another.

It is not that the facts themselves altered, for they are recorded imperishably in the monuments and in the pages of human history. But the interpretation to be put upon the facts underwent a change. Somehow the perspective shifted—not suddenly, as in a flash of insight or inspiration, but slowly, almost imperceptibly, by the very stubbornness of the facts themselves.

The book as it was originally planned was left high and dry, like those Thames barges when the great river goes out to meet the incoming sea. The writer discovered one day that not only could he no longer write the book as he had once conceived it, but that he would not if he could.

To tell the story of that change, and to give the reasons for it, is the main purpose of the following pages.

The Person and Work of the Holy Spirit
R. A. Torrey

Before one can correctly understand the work of the Holy Spirit, he must first of all know the Spirit Himself. A frequent source of error and fanaticism about the work of the Holy Spirit is the attempt to study and understand His work without first of all coming to know Him as a Person.

It is of the highest importance from the standpoint of worship that we decide whether the Holy Spirit is a Divine Person, worthy to receive our adoration, our faith, our love, and our entire surrender to Himself, or whether it is simply an influence emanating from God or a power or an illumination that God imparts to us. If the Holy Spirit is a person, and a Divine Person, and we do not know Him as such, then we are robbing a Divine Being of the worship and the faith and the love and the surrender to Himself which are His due.

In His Steps
Charles M. Sheldon

The sermon story, In His Steps, or "What Would Jesus Do?" was first written in the winter of 1896, and read by the author, a chapter at a time, to his Sunday evening congregation in the

Central Congregational Church, Topeka, Kansas. It was then printed as a serial in The Advance (Chicago), and its reception by the readers of that paper was such that the publishers of The Advance made arrangements for its appearance in book form. It was their desire, in which the author heartily joined, that the story might reach as many readers as possible, hence succeeding editions of paper-covered volumes at a price within the reach of nearly all readers.

The story has been warmly and thoughtfully welcomed by Endeavor societies, temperance organizations, and Y. M. C. A. 's. It is the earnest prayer of the author that the book may go its way with a great blessing to the churches for the quickening of Christian discipleship, and the hastening of the Master's kingdom on earth.

Printed in Great Britain
by Amazon